ALASKA

CRUISE

TRAVEL GUIDE 2024-2025

The Complete Handbook for First-Timers to
Explore the Colors of Alaskan Beauty, Covering
Ports, Top Destinations, What to Eat and Do, and
Other Attractions

Rick M. Driver

Disclaimer

Copyright © by Rick M. Driver 2024
All rights reserved.

Table Of Contents

Map of Seattle

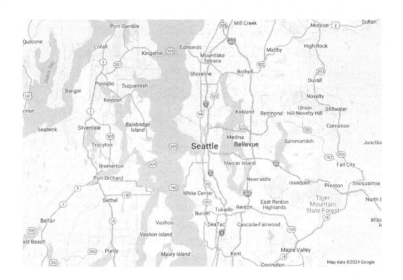

Introduction

In the northernmost realms of America, where rugged landscapes meet icy waters, a group of adventurous souls found themselves captivated by the allure of the great Alaskan wilderness. Their guide through this untamed odyssey was none other than the "Alaska Cruise Travel Guide."

Setting sail from the vibrant city of Seattle, the travelers eagerly delved into the guide's pages, discovering a narrative as vast and majestic as the landscapes it described. The journey unfolded along the enchanting Inside Passage, where emerald waters framed dense forests and jagged peaks stood sentinel in the distance.

In the bustling port of Juneau, the guide led them to the monumental Mendenhall Glacier, its icy expanse a testament to nature's grandeur. Further along the route, the vibrant town of Ketchikan revealed its cultural treasures, from intricately carved totem poles to the hustle and bustle of the salmon-filled air.

Navigating through the icy waters of Glacier Bay National Park, the guide directed their gaze to the monumental Hubbard Glacier, a living testament to the power and beauty of the natural world. Onboard experiences unfolded with the guide offering tips on

wildlife spotting and the art of capturing Alaska's
ethereal beauty through the lens.

Beyond the ship's decks, the guide extended its
influence to land adventures, guiding the travelers
through Denali National Park's vast wilderness and
Anchorage's harmonious blend of urban
sophistication and rugged landscapes.

In every chapter, the "Alaska Cruise Travel Guide"
not only provided practical advice but also wove
tales of indigenous cultures, urging the travelers to
respect and honor the rich traditions of Alaska's
native peoples. It became more than a guidebook; it
became a companion, shaping their journey into an
extraordinary story etched into the very fabric of
Alaska's wild heart. And so, beneath the dancing
lights of the aurora, the travelers discovered that the
most profound stories are written not just in

landscapes but in the hearts of those who embrace the call of the Last Frontier.

Chapter 1: Overview Of Alaska

History of Alaska

Alaska has a rich and complex history that spans thousands of years. The region was originally inhabited by various indigenous peoples, including the Inupiat, Yupik, Tlingit, Haida, and Athabascan peoples. These groups lived off the land, hunting, fishing, and gathering in the vast and often harsh Alaskan environment.

The first recorded European contact with Alaska was in 1741 when the Russian explorer Vitus Bering arrived on the coast of the Alaskan mainland. This led to a period of Russian exploration and exploitation of the region's resources, particularly fur-bearing animals. Russian settlers established trading posts and colonies, and by the early 19th century, Russia had firmly established its presence in Alaska.

In 1867, Russia agreed to sell Alaska to the United States for $7.2 million in a deal known as the Alaska Purchase. During that period, the purchase faced widespread criticism in the United States, earning the moniker "Seward's Folly" in reference to Secretary of State William H. Seward, but it ultimately proved to be a highly strategic acquisition. Alaska transitioned from Russian to U.S. control on October 18, 1867.

After the purchase, the U.S. government struggled to effectively govern and develop the vast territory. The discovery of gold in the late 19th century brought an influx of settlers to Alaska, leading to increased economic activity and development. The Klondike Gold Rush of 1896-1899, which drew prospectors to the Yukon region in Canada, also had a significant impact on Alaska's development.

During World War II, Alaska became a crucial military outpost due to its proximity to Asia. The construction of military bases and infrastructure during this time had a lasting impact on the state's economy and demographics.

In 1959, Alaska officially became the 49th state of the United States of America. The discovery of oil on Alaska's North Slope in the 1960s brought further economic development to the state, but also raised environmental concerns and led to debates over land use and conservation.

Alaska's history is also marked by the struggle for indigenous rights and recognition. The Alaska Native Claims Settlement Act of 1971 resulted in the largest land claims settlement in U.S. history, granting indigenous groups ownership of millions of acres of land and establishing regional and village corporations to manage these lands and resources.

Today, Alaska is known for its stunning natural beauty, diverse wildlife, and unique cultural heritage. The state's history continues to shape its identity and plays a central role in its ongoing social, economic, and political dynamics.

Culture and Etiquette

Culture:

The state of Alaska is known for its continuing frontier spirit, along with Russian and indigenous traditions, which combine to create a captivating cultural tapestry. Deeply ingrained in traditional traditions such as subsistence hunting, fishing, and gathering, the cultural landscape of the region is anchored by numerous Native Alaskan communities, including the Inupiat, Yupik, and

Athabascan. Native American art forms in Alaska include elaborate carvings, colorful beading, and symbolic totem poles, which are visual representations of the peoples' relationship to the land and its resources.

Alaska was a Russian territory until the United States purchased it in 1867, leaving a Russian legacy that adds a unique element to the state's cultural mosaic. Churches such as St. Michael's Cathedral in Sitka are testaments to the enduring impact of Russian Orthodox Christianity; other examples of Russian influence can be found in specific architectural designs and culinary customs.

Alaskans are still shaped by the persistent frontier spirit that was fostered during the Gold Rush. Self-reliance, tenacity, and a "can-do" mentality—all essential for surviving in the harsh and difficult surroundings—define this character. Dog sledding and ice fishing are just two examples of the outdoor activities that highlight Alaskans' love of the outdoors and their spirit of adventure.

A number of cultural gatherings and festivals that provide platforms for people of all backgrounds to exhibit their traditions are used to honor Alaska's diversity. People are encouraged to value and accept the diversity of cultural backgrounds that make up Alaskan identity because of the atmosphere this openness fosters.

Notwithstanding the celebration of Alaska's cultural diversity, the state also faces problems with social difficulties, economic shifts, and climate change. These difficulties, which have a special effect on indigenous groups, force them to make constant adjustments in an effort to maintain their customs amidst a setting that is changing quickly.

Etiquette:

Alaskan etiquette is a nuanced blend of indigenous customs, frontier traditions, and contemporary social norms. While there are no stringent rules governing behavior, cultural norms and practices are generally observed, contributing to a harmonious coexistence in this vast and diverse state.

Respect for nature is a foundational element of Alaskan etiquette, with a deep reverence for the natural environment and wildlife. Outdoor activities, such as hiking, camping, and fishing, are guided by Leave No Trace principles, emphasizing minimal impact and conservation efforts.

Hospitality in this city is renowned for its warmth and friendliness. Greetings are often accompanied by a genuine smile and a welcoming demeanor. Visitors to rural communities should be prepared to show respect for local customs and traditions, further fostering a sense of community.

Outdoor etiquette extends to activities like fishing or hunting, emphasizing adherence to local regulations and obtaining necessary permits or licenses. It also underscores the importance of respecting property rights and seeking permission before accessing private land.

Cultural sensitivity is paramount when interacting with Alaska Native communities. Visitors are encouraged to learn about the customs and protocols of the specific community they are visiting, demonstrating respect for their cultural practices and traditions.

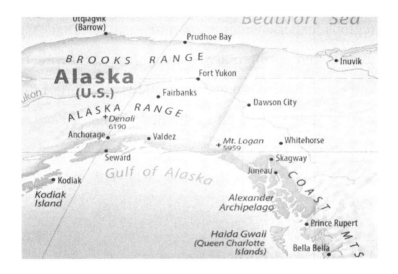

Geography

Alaska is known to be largest state in the United States of America, covering an expanse exceeding 663,000 square miles. It is located in the northwest corner of North America, bordered by Canada to the east and the Pacific Ocean to the west. The state includes significant islands, such as the Aleutian Islands, and is home to numerous rivers and lakes, including the mighty Yukon River and Lake Iliamna. Alaska's climate varies widely, with southern coastal regions experiencing a maritime climate and the interior and northern areas having long, cold winters and short, cool summers. The state is also part of the Pacific Ring of Fire and is home to numerous active volcanoes.

Landscapes

The landscape of Alaska is characterized by vast, untamed wilderness, dramatic mountain ranges, expansive tundra, and abundant waterways.

Prominent mountain ranges include the iconic Alaska Range with Denali, the highest mountain in North America, as well as the Brooks Range, Chugach Mountains, and Coast Mountains. Alaska boasts an impressive array of glaciers, including the Hubbard Glacier, Mendenhall Glacier, and Columbia Glacier. The northern regions are covered by vast expanses of tundra, while dense boreal forests dominate much of the interior and southern parts of the state. Alaska's extensive coastline is marked by fjords, rugged cliffs, and pristine beaches, with coastal waters teeming with marine life.

Languages Spoken in Alaska

Alaska is a multilingual state whose significant linguistic diversity reflects the state's rich cultural legacy. Its indigenous languages include Tlingit-Haida, Athabaskan, and Eskimo-Aleut, which are divided into multiple linguistic groups. Inupiaq, Siberian Yupik, Central Alaskan Yup'ik, and Alutiiq are spoken in the north and west, whereas Athabaskan languages are more common in interior and southeast Alaska. The Tlingit and Haida peoples of southeast Alaska speak Tlingit and Haida languages. In addition to their original tongues, many Alaskans speak English as a second language. It is the most common language used for government reasons. Languages spoken in the Pacific Islands, including Spanish, Tagalog, Korean, and Russian, have also been introduced to the state by immigrant communities.

In Alaska, efforts to protect native tongues are important. Through immersion programs, revitalization projects, and educational materials, organizations such as the Alaska Native Language Center and tribal language programs strive to document, teach, and promote indigenous languages. One other piece of legislation supporting continuous efforts to preserve language variety in the state is the Alaska Native Claims Settlement Act of 1971. All things considered, Alaska's linguistic landscape serves as evidence of the state's rich cultural heritage and the need of protecting and advancing native tongues.

Useful Slangs and Phrases for First timers In Alaska

- Bush - Remote, rural areas
- Lower 48 - The contiguous United States
- Sled - Snowmobile
- Moose nugget - A term of endearment or a way to refer to someone from Alaska
- Cheechako - A newcomer to Alaska
- Sourtoe - A shot of alcohol with a preserved human toe in it, a tradition in Dawson City, Yukon Territory (popular with Alaskans)

- The Last Frontier - Alaska's nickname
- The Great Land - Another nickname for Alaska
- Fish camp - A temporary residence near a fishing area
- Breakup - The spring thaw when ice and snow melt
- Mushing - Traveling by dog sled
- Tundra - The treeless plains in the Arctic and subarctic regions
- Ice road - A temporary road made of ice for winter travel
- Bush plane - Small aircraft used for transportation in remote areas
- Dipnetting - Using a large net to catch fish from rivers
- Termination dust - The first snowfall that signals the end of summer
- Midnight sun - The phenomenon of the sun not setting during the summer months

- Northern lights - The Aurora Borealis, a natural light display in the Arctic and Antarctic regions
- Big dipper - The constellation visible throughout the year in Alaska
- Chilkoot - A steep mountain pass in southeastern Alaska
- Gold rush - Refers to the historical gold mining boom in Alaska and the Yukon Territory
- Totem pole - Carved wooden poles depicting symbols and stories of indigenous peoples
- Fur Rondy - An annual winter festival in Anchorage
- Iditarod - A famous long-distance sled dog race from Anchorage to Nome
- Kodiak bear - A subspecies of brown bear found on Kodiak Island
- Sourdough - A long-time resident of Alaska

- Klondike - Refers to the Klondike Gold Rush in the late 1800s
- Blueberry picking - A popular summer activity in Alaska
- Grizzly - Another term for brown bear
- Caribou - A species of wild reindeer found in Alaska
- Ice fishing - Fishing through holes cut in frozen lakes or rivers
- Snowmachine - Another term for a snowmobile
- Subsistence living - Living off the land, often through hunting and gathering
- Northern pike - A predatory fish found in Alaskan waters
- Ice fishing derby - A competition for catching fish through the ice

Chapter 2: Getting Started

When to Cruise Alaska

There are a number of elements to take into account when deciding when is the best time to take an Alaskan cruise. The cruise season normally runs from late spring to early fall, with May through September being the main window. Temperatures in late spring, especially in May and early June, vary from 40°F to 60°F (4°C to 15°C). Alaska starts to emerge from its winter hibernation around this time of year. Vibrant wildflowers bloom and the remaining snow creates a stunning backdrop. It's a season when animals come out to feed, providing chances to see bears, eagles, and whales that are migrating.

As the season progresses into summer, from mid-June to August, the peak of Alaska's cruise season unfolds. This period brings milder temperatures, ranging from 60°F to 70°F (15°C to 21°C), making it an ideal time for cruising. One of the highlights of an Alaska summer cruise is the extended daylight hours, allowing for more time to explore and witness the breathtaking scenery. Wildlife is abundant, with whales, bears, seals, and various seabirds making appearances, often showcasing fascinating behaviors, and the summer months also coincide with the annual salmon runs.

The end of the cruise season is marked by the transition into early fall, especially in September. As the temperature drops to between 40°F and 60°F (4°C and 15°C), the landscape is colored in shades of red, orange, and yellow by the fall foliage. The wildlife is still in motion, offering an opportunity to watch animals getting ready for winter. Furthermore, September offers the chance to see the Northern Lights, which are a captivating celestial show.

When to take an Alaskan cruise ultimately comes down to personal tastes. A more sedate experience with fewer tourists and changing seasonal scenery can be had in late spring or early fall, while the summer months give the best opportunities for milder temperatures, longer days, and plenty of wildlife viewing. Alaska is an enthralling location all year round since each season has its own distinct charm.

Key Ports and Destinations

Alaska captures the hearts of cruise travelers with its awe-inspiring landscapes, diverse wildlife, and a wealth of cultural experiences. The ports and destinations on an Alaska cruise showcase the state's untamed beauty, offering a range of activities from glacier exploration and wildlife encounters to historical immersions. Here's an overview of some key ports and destinations often featured in Alaska cruise itineraries:

Juneau

As the capital of Alaska, Juneau is a common stop on many Alaska cruises. Visitors to Juneau can explore the Mendenhall Glacier, a stunning natural wonder located just 12 miles from downtown. Additionally, the city offers opportunities for whale watching, hiking, and visiting the Alaska State Museum to learn about the region's history and culture.

Skagway

Skagway is known for its rich Gold Rush history and well-preserved downtown area, which transports visitors back to the late 19th century. While in Skagway, cruise passengers can take a historic train ride on the White Pass and Yukon Route Railroad, explore the Klondike Gold Rush National Historical Park, or leave on outdoor activities like hiking and zip-lining.

Ketchikan

Ketchikan is often referred to as the "Salmon Capital of the World" and is famous for its totem poles and Native American culture. Visitors can witness traditional Native Alaskan dance performances, visit the Totem Bight State Historical Park, or take a guided tour through the Tongass National Forest. Additionally, Ketchikan offers opportunities for bear watching, fishing, and exploring Misty Fjords National Monument.

Sitka

Sitka is a picturesque town with a rich Russian and Tlingit heritage. Visitors can explore historical sites such as the Russian Bishop's House and St. Michael's Cathedral, as well as enjoy outdoor activities like kayaking, wildlife viewing, and hiking in the nearby Tongass National Forest.

Glacier Bay National Park

Many Alaska cruises include a visit to Glacier Bay National Park, a UNESCO World Heritage Site renowned for its stunning glaciers, fjords, and diverse wildlife. Visitors can witness calving glaciers, spot humpback whales and sea lions, and admire the park's breathtaking natural beauty from the comfort of their cruise ship.

Hubbard Glacier

Hubbard Glacier is another popular destination on Alaska cruises, offering passengers the chance to witness one of the most active glaciers in North America. Cruisers can marvel at the towering ice formations and listen for the dramatic sounds of ice breaking off into the sea.

These are just a few examples of the many ports and destinations that may be included in an Alaska cruise itinerary. Each destination offers its own unique blend of natural beauty, cultural experiences, and outdoor adventures, making an Alaska cruise an unforgettable journey through one of the world's most awe-inspiring regions.

Sea Temperature

The sea temperature on an Alaska cruise can vary widely depending on the specific location, time of year, and prevailing weather conditions. Generally, the sea temperature in Alaska's coastal waters ranges from around 40°F (4°C) to 55°F (13°C) during the peak summer months. However, it's important to note that these temperatures are averages and can fluctuate significantly based on various factors such as ocean currents, proximity to glaciers, and local weather patterns.

During the early summer months, particularly May and June, sea temperatures tend to be at their coolest, often hovering around the lower end of the spectrum, between 40°F to 45°F (4°C to 7°C). This is due to the lingering effects of winter and the gradual warming of the ocean as the summer progresses. As the season progresses into July and August, sea temperatures typically rise, reaching the upper end of the range, between 50°F to 55°F (10°C to 13°C).

When taking an Alaskan cruise, the sea's temperature may also change in certain interesting locations. For instance, the presence of glacial meltwater can considerably reduce the overall temperature of the surrounding ocean, resulting in colder sea temperatures in coastal areas close to glaciers. Furthermore, sea temperatures may be lower in northern regions—such as those around Glacier Bay and the Inside Passage—than in southern regions, such as Ketchikan or Juneau.

A cruise's overall experience is greatly influenced by the sea's temperature. If passengers intend to partake in activities like kayaking, animal viewing, or even swimming in specific regions, they should be ready for colder water temperatures. Depending on the current sea temperatures, the cruise line may offer advice on what to wear and how to take safety precautions when participating in water sports.

The moderating effect of ocean currents and seasonal warming means that although sea temperatures in Alaska may be lower than in more tropical locations, they can still vary greatly and may not be as low as one might anticipate. By packing appropriately for their Alaskan cruise, travelers can ensure a comfortable and happy time while experiencing this stunning region. This can be achieved by being aware of the sea temperature.

Flora And Fauna in Alaska

In the vast and varied landscapes of the region, a tremendous diversity of flora and fauna thrives within the ecosystem. The unique and untamed wilderness fosters an exceptional haven for numerous plant and animal species. From rugged coasts to lofty mountains, the diverse ecosystems contribute to the vibrant natural fabric of this area. The interplay of different habitats creates a captivating environment, allowing a rich array of life to flourish in both flora and fauna.

Flora:

Embarking on an Alaska cruise unveils the striking plant life along its shores. Lining the coastal areas are dense forests featuring towering Sitka spruce, western red cedar, and western hemlock trees. In the southeastern part of Alaska, the lush coastal rainforests are enriched with ferns, mosses, lichens, and vibrant wildflowers like skunk cabbage, devil's club, and blueberry bushes.

Further north, the cruise may take you to the tundra regions, characterized by low-growing vegetation including grasses, sedges, mosses, lichens, and hardy flowering plants like Arctic poppies, mountain avens, and purple saxifrage.

The Inside Passage and Gulf of Alaska introduce expanses of boreal forests with coniferous trees like spruce, fir, and pine, interspersed with deciduous species such as aspen, birch, and willow.

Fauna:

The marine environment along the Alaska coast is a highlight, providing ample opportunities to witness the majesty of marine mammals. Humpback whales make a grand entrance, breaching and slapping their tails with breathtaking precision. Orcas, or killer whales, showcase their predatory prowess, creating a thrilling spectacle for onlookers. Playful sea otters float serenely on their backs, while Steller sea lions, the giants of the sea, bask on rocky outcrops, adding a touch of drama to the coastal scenery. The annual migration of gray whales, a testament to the wonders of nature, may be a fortunate encounter, leaving a lasting impression on lucky cruise-goers.

Bird enthusiasts are in for a treat as the cruise navigates through Alaska's coastal waters and islands. Bald eagles, with their iconic white heads, soar overhead, their keen eyes scanning the surroundings. Puffins, with their comical appearance, find refuge on rocky cliffs, while common murres dive with remarkable precision to secure their underwater prey. Marbled murrelets contribute to the avian symphony by skimming the water's surface, creating a dynamic and lively atmosphere. Gulls, terns, and cormorants join this coastal ballet, enhancing the rich diversity of birdlife that accompanies the cruise.

The nutrient-rich waters of Alaska support a thriving community of fish species, and their presence is integral to the region's ecosystem. Bald eagles become aerial acrobats, swooping down with precision to snatch salmon from the water, showcasing a remarkable display of nature's interconnectedness. Sea lions, with agility and speed, actively hunt for their next meal, creating an engaging spectacle for those on deck. Schools of salmon, a vital component of this aquatic realm, swim near the surface, and the occasional breach of these remarkable fish adds to the maritime excitement.

On land, Alaska's rugged beauty is complemented by an array of mammals, each adapted to its unique habitat. Black bears, with their distinctive fur, may be observed foraging along the shoreline, while mountain goats scale steep cliffs with astonishing agility, particularly in areas like Glacier Bay National Park. The wooded areas surrounding the cruise route provide a habitat for mammals such as otters, beavers, and deer. Smaller creatures, including frogs, toads, and insects, thrive in the wetlands and marshes, contributing to the intricate balance of this terrestrial ecosystem.

The glacial landscapes of Alaska unveil a unique facet of wildlife. Harbor seals find refuge on ice floes near tidewater glaciers, their sleek forms contrasting against the icy backdrop. Arctic terns and other seabirds, resilient and adaptable, may be spotted nesting on rocky outcrops near glacier fronts, further enriching the biodiversity of this awe-inspiring region.

In addition to its wild inhabitants, Alaska's cruise experience may also offer glimpses of domesticated animals, showcasing the harmonious coexistence of human life with the untamed beauty of the Alaskan wilderness. An Alaska cruise promises a holistic encounter with nature's wonders, where every fjord, forest, and glacier becomes a stage for the captivating drama of wildlife.

Chapter 3: Preparing for the Cruise

Choosing The Right Cruise Lines

There are a few things to take into account while selecting the best cruise line for an Alaskan vacation. Knowing the distinctions between each cruise line's offerings can help you choose the one that most closely matches your tastes and manner of travel. The following are important factors to take into account while selecting the best cruise line for your Alaskan adventure:

1. Itinerary and Ports of Call:

Different cruise lines may offer varying itineraries and visit different ports of call in Alaska. Consider the specific destinations you want to visit, such as Glacier Bay, Hubbard Glacier, Juneau, Ketchikan, Skagway, or Sitka. Some cruise lines may also include additional stops in Canada or other parts of the Pacific Northwest.

2. Ship Size and Style:

Cruise lines operate ships of varying sizes and styles. Larger ships often offer more onboard amenities and entertainment options, while smaller ships may provide a more intimate and personalized experience. Consider whether you prefer the bustling atmosphere of a larger vessel or the more serene ambiance of a smaller ship.

3. Onboard Activities and Entertainment:

Each cruise line offers a distinct array of onboard activities and entertainment options. Whether you're interested in Broadway-style shows, educational lectures about Alaska's wildlife and culture, culinary experiences, or outdoor activities like kayaking and hiking, it's important to choose a cruise line that aligns with your interests.

4. Dining Options:

Think about the dining options that each cruise line presents. Some lines are known for their gourmet cuisine and specialty restaurants, while others may focus on casual dining experiences or regional cuisine that highlights local flavors and ingredients.

5. Shore Excursions:

Research the shore excursions available through each cruise line. Whether you're interested in wildlife viewing, glacier trekking, dog sledding, or cultural tours, ensure that the cruise line offers excursions that match your interests and activity level.

6. Onboard Enrichment Programs:

Some cruise lines provide onboard enrichment programs that focus on the natural and cultural history of Alaska. These programs may include expert-led lectures, photography workshops, and interactive experiences designed to deepen your understanding of the region.

7. Environmental Stewardship:

Consider the cruise line's commitment to environmental stewardship and sustainable practices. Some cruise lines have implemented initiatives to minimize their environmental impact in Alaska, such as reducing emissions, supporting local conservation efforts, and implementing responsible wildlife viewing guidelines.

8. Family-Friendly Amenities:

If you're traveling with children or teenagers, consider the family-friendly amenities offered by each cruise line. Look for age-appropriate kids' clubs, teen centers, family-friendly shore excursions, and onboard activities designed for families.

9. Budget and Value:

Compare the pricing and value offered by different cruise lines. Take into account the overall cost of the cruise, including accommodations, meals, onboard activities, gratuities, and any additional expenses such as alcoholic beverages, spa services, and shore excursions.

10. Reputation and Reviews:

Research the reputation and customer reviews of each cruise line. Online travel forums, review websites, and recommendations from friends or travel agents can provide valuable insights into the quality of service, onboard experience, and overall satisfaction of past passengers.

Cruise Types and Prices

Alaska is a magnificent state that offers a wide variety of cruise experiences. Its unmatched natural beauty captivates travelers. Every traveler can find a new and interesting journey with the variety of cruise alternatives available in this vast and wild area, each one appealing to different interests and preferences. Time to explore the wide variety of Alaskan cruises, which fall into five main categories.

Inside Passage Cruises

Embarking on an Inside Passage cruise unveils a mesmerizing journey through the protected waterways, offering panoramic vistas of fjords, glaciers, and lush forests. Departing from ports like Seattle, Vancouver, or Seward, these cruises navigate through iconic destinations such as Juneau, Skagway, and Ketchikan. Passengers encounter the untamed wildlife of Alaska, including whales, sea lions, and bears. Excursions may include whale watching, exploring the Mendenhall Glacier, or embarking on a historic train ride, crafting an immersive experience into the region's history and natural wonders. Prices for Inside Passage Cruises typically range from $1,500 to $5,000 per person, depending on the cruise line, duration, and cabin category.

Glacier Cruises

For those enchanted by the ethereal beauty of glaciers, Alaska's Glacier Cruises focus on exploring renowned sites like Glacier Bay National Park and Hubbard Glacier. Guided by park rangers or naturalists, passengers gain profound insights into the geological marvels, diverse flora, and fauna of the region. Witnessing the awe-inspiring spectacle of calving glaciers, where colossal ice chunks break off into the water, is a highlight. Hubbard Glacier, with its dramatic calving events, stands as a testament to the dynamic forces shaping Alaska's icy landscapes. Prices for Glacier Cruises typically range from $2,000 to $6,000 per person, depending on the cruise line, duration, and cabin category.

Expedition Cruises

Designed for the intrepid traveler, Expedition Cruises offer a more immersive and adventurous experience. Navigating on smaller ships and yachts, these cruises provide opportunities for kayaking, hiking, and encounters with polar bears and whales. Access to remote and less-explored areas enables passengers to witness Alaska's pristine natural beauty, wildlife, and indigenous cultures up close. Excursions may include visits to isolated coastal communities, exploration of hidden coves, and the observation of rare bird species, creating an unparalleled sense of discovery. Prices for Expedition Cruises typically range from $3,000 to $8,000 per person, depending on the cruise line, duration, and cabin category.

Wildlife and Nature Cruises

Alaska's Wildlife and Nature Cruises prioritize connecting passengers with the rich biodiversity of the region. Focused on encounters with iconic wildlife like bald eagles, brown bears, otters, and marine mammals, these cruises feature naturalist guides who impart ecological insights and conservation awareness. Guests partake in wildlife-viewing expeditions, enhancing their understanding of Alaska's delicate ecosystems. These cruises contribute to a deeper appreciation for the interconnectedness of the flora and fauna in this rugged wilderness. Prices for Wildlife and Nature Cruises typically range from $2,500 to $7,000 per person, depending on the cruise line, duration, and cabin category.

Luxury Cruises

For those desiring the epitome of comfort and opulence, Luxury Cruises in Alaska offer an exquisite blend of premium amenities, gourmet dining, and personalized service against the backdrop of Alaska's awe-inspiring landscapes. These high-end cruises boast spacious suites, upscale amenities, and exclusive shore excursions, allowing guests to explore the state's attractions in unparalleled comfort. Some options include private balconies for glacier viewing, onboard spas, and gourmet cooking demonstrations by renowned chefs, providing an indulgent experience amidst the untamed beauty of Alaska. Prices for Luxury Cruises typically range from $5,000 to $15,000 or more per person, depending on the cruise line, duration, and cabin category.

Best Cruise Lines With Budgeting

Many respectable options accommodate different tastes and budgets for people thinking about taking an Alaskan cruise. Considerations including cost, onboard amenities, itinerary highlights, and the makeup of your travel party should all be taken into account when choosing the best cruise lines for your Alaskan excursion. The following renowned cruise lines are available for trips to Alaska:

Norwegian Cruise Line

Norwegian Cruise Line stands out for its diverse array of budget-friendly options designed specifically for Alaska cruises. The fleet boasts an impressive range of amenities and entertainment choices, complemented by frequent special promotions and deals tailored for Alaska-bound travelers. The flexibility of dining arrangements ensures that guests can savor their culinary experiences at a pace that aligns with both their preferences and budget. Prices for Norwegian cruises to Alaska typically start at $600 per person and may vary based on the chosen itinerary and cabin type.

Princess Cruises

Renowned for its affordable Alaska cruise options, Princess Cruises delivers a spectrum of itineraries catering to diverse budgets. The cruise line's vessels are well-appointed with a myriad of onboard activities and entertainment options, ensuring passengers experience a well-rounded voyage. An additional highlight is Princess Cruises' "North to Alaska" program, which seamlessly integrates local culinary and cultural experiences into the journey, enriching the adventure at no extra cost. Prices for Princess Cruises Alaska cruises usually begin around $700 per person, with variations based on the selected itinerary and cabin category.

Holland America Line

Holland America Line intricately weaves traditional cruising experiences into budget-friendly Alaska voyages. With an emphasis on elegant décor and a diverse range of dining options, including reasonably priced specialty restaurants, the cruise line offers a sophisticated yet affordable adventure. Holland America Line further enhances the exploration with cost-effective shore excursions that enable guests to immerse themselves in the natural splendor of Alaska. Prices for Holland America Line Alaska cruises typically start at $650 per person and may vary based on the chosen itinerary and cabin type.

Carnival Cruise Line

Carnival Cruise Line injects an element of affordability into Alaska cruising without compromising on the fun and lively atmosphere it is known for. The fleet's vessels are brimming with diverse onboard activities and entertainment, ranging from water parks to live shows and themed parties. Carnival Cruise Line extends its budget-friendly ethos to dining options, offering casual eateries and complimentary room service to suit a variety of tastes and financial plans. Prices for Carnival Cruise Line Alaska cruises generally start at $500 per person, with variations based on the selected itinerary and cabin category.

Royal Caribbean International

Royal Caribbean International elevates the Alaska cruising experience with budget-friendly options featuring innovative onboard amenities and entertainment. From rock climbing walls to ice skating rinks and Broadway-style shows, the cruise line ensures that guests have access to a plethora of entertainment without additional charges. Flexible dining options, including complimentary main dining rooms and casual eateries, further enhance the appeal of Royal Caribbean International for budget-conscious travelers. Prices for Royal Caribbean International Alaska cruises typically start at $550 per person and may vary based on the chosen itinerary and cabin type.

When embarking on the quest for a budget-friendly Alaska cruise, it becomes imperative to factor in additional costs like gratuities, shore excursions, and alcoholic beverages. Opting for cruise lines that provide inclusive packages or promotions covering these expenses can be a savvy financial move. Additionally, considering the advantages of booking during the shoulder season in May or September, when prices typically dip, or exploring last-minute deals, can contribute to substantial savings. In conclusion, the highlighted cruise lines present enticing options for an Alaska cruise that align with various budgetary considerations. By thoughtfully weighing your financial parameters and leveraging available promotions and packages, an unforgettable Alaskan adventure can be embarked upon without causing a strain on your wallet.

Travel Insurance

Travel insurance must be carefully considered before embarking on an Alaskan cruise due to the vast and isolated terrain of the area, as well as the possibility of erratic weather and wildlife sightings.

There are a number of reasons why purchasing travel insurance is essential. First of all, it provides coverage for trip cancellation and interruption, guarding against last-minute changes or cancellations brought on by illness, accidents, or urgent family matters. This guarantees payment for non-refundable costs like airfare, cruise tickets, and scheduled excursions.

The remote and expansive wilderness of Alaska emphasizes the importance of emergency medical coverage, which provides solace in the event of sickness or mishap when cruising. This includes medical attention, evacuation transportation to suitable facilities, and, if necessary, repatriation. Evacuation and repatriation coverage, which pays for emergency air or sea evacuations, becomes crucial to overcoming the challenges posed by Alaska's ecosystems.

Furthermore, additional costs incurred as a result of delays or missed connections are reimbursed by the Travel Delay and Missed Connection Coverage, providing financial security for lodging, meals, and travel. Baggage Loss and Delay Coverage guarantees reimbursement for necessary items in the event that baggage is misplaced, stolen, or delayed.

Flexibility is increased with Cancel for Any Reason (CFAR) Coverage, which enables passengers to recover a portion of their non-refundable trip expenses for causes that aren't usually covered by regular plans. Buyers should carefully research the specifics of the policy, taking into account things like coverage limits, exclusions, pre-existing condition restrictions, and claims procedures, in order to make an informed choice.

To guarantee coverage for unanticipated incidents, it is advised to purchase insurance as soon as the cruise is booked. Comparing insurance from reliable companies is essential to obtaining the best coverage for a trip to Alaska. In the end, travel insurance reduces the dangers connected with distant and adventurous travel in Alaska and offers priceless financial protection and peace of mind.

Money Saving Tips

Travelers can maximize their Alaskan cruise experience without going over budget by following these money-saving suggestions. Here are some thorough methods for cutting costs while taking advantage of everything an Alaskan cruise has to offer:

1. Book Early or Last Minute:

Booking your Alaska cruise well in advance or at the last minute can often result in significant savings. Cruise lines often offer early booking discounts and promotions, as well as last-minute deals to fill remaining cabins. Keep an eye on cruise line websites, travel agencies, and deal-finding websites to snag the best prices.

2. Consider Shoulder Season or Off-Peak Dates:

Alaska's cruise season typically runs from May to September, with peak demand during the summer months. Consider traveling during the shoulder season (May or September) to take advantage of lower prices and fewer crowds while still enjoying the stunning scenery and wildlife.

3.   Research   Port   Excursions Independently:

While shore excursions offered by the cruise line can be convenient, they often come with a premium price tag. Research and book excursions independently through local tour operators or explore on your own to save money. Many ports in Alaska offer opportunities for self-guided hikes, wildlife viewing, and cultural experiences at a fraction of the cost of organized tours.

4. Bring Your Own Beverages:

Most cruise lines allow passengers to bring a limited amount of their own beverages on board, such as wine or non-alcoholic drinks. Check the cruise line's policy on bringing beverages and take advantage of this to save on expensive onboard drink prices.

5. Take Advantage of Onboard Dining Options:

While specialty restaurants on cruise ships can offer a more upscale dining experience, the main dining rooms and buffet options often provide delicious meals included in the cruise fare. Take advantage of these options to avoid additional dining expenses.

6. Pack Wisely:

Avoid unnecessary expenses by packing smartly for your Alaska cruise. Bring essential items such as rain gear, layers for varying temperatures, and binoculars for wildlife viewing, as purchasing these items onboard or in port can be costly.

7. Look for Package Deals:

Some cruise lines offer package deals that bundle amenities such as drink packages, Wi-Fi, or onboard credit with the cruise fare. Research these options to determine if they provide savings compared to purchasing these items separately.

8. Monitor Onboard Spending:

Set a budget for onboard spending and monitor your expenses throughout the cruise. Be mindful of additional costs for activities, spa services, shopping, and gratuities to avoid overspending.

9. Utilize Loyalty Programs or Discounts:

If you've cruised with a particular line before or have memberships with travel organizations, check for loyalty program benefits or discounts that can help reduce the overall cost of your Alaska cruise.

10. Be Flexible with Cabin Selection:

Consider opting for an inside cabin or a room with a partially obstructed view to save on accommodation costs. Since much of the allure of an Alaska cruise lies in the outdoor scenery, you may find that a pricier cabin with a full view is not essential.

Internet And Wifi Availability Onboard

Access to the internet and Wi-Fi while on a cruise through Alaska might vary depending on a number of factors, including the cruise line, ship, and itinerary. Passengers' connectivity options are made more challenging by the vast and remote character of Alaska's coastal seas. We delve into the complexities of internet and Wi-Fi access on Alaska cruises in this in-depth investigation.

1. Internet Access Options:

Satellite Internet: The predominant method for providing internet connectivity at sea is through satellite technology. However, due to the remoteness of Alaska's coastal waters, passengers may experience slower and less reliable internet speeds compared to more populated regions.

Onboard Internet Cafes: Some cruise ships offer designated internet cafes where passengers can access the internet either through shipboard computers or their personal devices. These areas may have specific operational hours and could involve additional charges for usage.

2. Wi-Fi Availability:

Shipwide Wi-Fi: Many modern cruise ships have wide Wi-Fi coverage, enabling passengers to connect to the internet from various areas such as staterooms, public spaces, and outdoor decks. Nevertheless, Wi-Fi availability may be constrained or intermittent in the remote expanses of Alaskan waters.

Wi-Fi Hotspots: Specific locations on the ship, such as lounges, restaurants, and designated Wi-Fi zones, may provide stronger signals for passengers seeking internet connectivity.

3. Internet Packages and Pricing:

Pay-Per-Use: Some cruise lines offer pay-per-use internet plans, where passengers are charged based on the time or data consumed. This option provides flexibility for those who only require occasional internet access.

Unlimited Packages: Alternatively, cruise lines may present unlimited internet packages for a fixed fee, offering continuous connectivity without concerns about overage charges.

Pre-Cruise Packages: Some cruise lines allow passengers to purchase internet packages before embarking on the cruise, often at a discounted rate compared to onboard prices.

4. Considerations for Internet Use:

Bandwidth Limitations: The shared nature of satellite internet on a cruise ship may lead to bandwidth constraints, resulting in slower speeds during peak usage times or in remote areas.

Data-Intensive Activities: Engaging in data-intensive activities such as streaming video or downloading large files may prove impractical or cost-ineffective due to potential limitations on speed and data usage.

5. Tips for Using Internet and Wi-Fi:

Manage Expectations: Given the remote and rugged characteristics of Alaska's coastal regions, passengers are advised to manage expectations regarding internet speed and reliability.

Plan Ahead: For those for whom staying connected is crucial, considerations include purchasing an internet package before the cruise or exploring alternative options for internet access in port cities.

Monitor Usage: To avoid unexpected charges, passengers should monitor internet usage and exercise caution with data-intensive activities that may deplete allotted data allowances quickly.

6. Offshore Connectivity:

In Port Wi-Fi: When the ship is docked in port cities along the Alaskan coast, passengers may have opportunities to access free or paid Wi-Fi services at local establishments, visitor centers, or tourist attractions.

Cellular Roaming: Depending on their mobile service provider and international roaming capabilities, passengers might use cellular devices to access data while in port. However, potential high international roaming fees necessitate checking with the provider beforehand.

Chapter 4: Food and Drink Options Offered Onboard

Set out on a culinary adventure through Alaska's wild landscapes, where every meal is a mouthwatering investigation of the region's unique flavors. The Alaska Cruise offers everything for every taste, from the warmth of hearty cuisine to the richness of wild-caught seafood, all while ensuring an excellent dining experience against the stunning backdrop of the Alaskan environment.

Give yourself over to the whole experience, not just the food. Imagine indulging in delectable meals while taking in the breathtaking views of snow-capped peaks and glaciers. It's about enjoying the true spirit of Alaska, not just a cruise.

The meals served on board are exquisite works of art, with each dish revealing a story that ties you to the customs and tastes of the Last Frontier. Every meal is a chance to delve further into Alaska's rich cultural diversity, whether it's a full breakfast, a relaxed lunch with a nod to the surrounding area, or a sophisticated supper with a fusion of cuisines.

The gastronomic selections become an inseparable part of the entire experience as the ship sails through the pure seas of the Alaskan wilderness. The beverage options available on board are made to satisfy a wide range of palates, from craft beers to locally inspired drinks. An Alaskan cruise is more than just a travel; it's a delectable culinary excursion with a multitude of flavors, cultural discoveries, and an authentic chance to sample regional food.

Foods To Expect:

Breakfast:

- Freshly Baked Alaskan Sourdough Bread and Pastries
- Wild Berries and Smoked Salmon
- Alaskan Crab Omelets
- Reindeer Sausages and Birch Syrup Pancakes
- Steel-Cut Oatmeal with Berry Compote
- Artisanal Alaskan Coffee and Herbal Teas

Lunch:

- Wild Mushroom Bisque
- Alaska King Crab Salad
- Grilled Salmon Tacos
- Halibut Chowder
- Caribou Sliders and Root Vegetable Fries
- Alaskan Berry Sorbet

Dinner:

- Alaskan Seafood Platter
- Juniper-Spiced Caribou Steak
- Salmon En Papillote
- Wild Berry Reduction Duck Breast
- Vegetarian Mountain Harvest Stew

Drinks To Expect:

- Alaskan Craft Beer Tasting
- Icy Blue Glacier Cocktails
- Wilderness Mint Tea and Spruce Tip Infusions
- Alaskan Birch Sap Sodas
- Crisp Glacial Water and Freshly Pressed Juices

Chapter 5: Things To Do Onboard

On an Alaska cruise, passengers can enjoy a wide variety of activities and amenities onboard, ranging from outdoor adventures to cultural experiences and relaxation. These are opportunities for passengers to make the most of their time at sea while enjoying the stunning scenery and unique offerings of an Alaskan voyage. Here are the detailed aspects of things to do onboard on an Alaska cruise:

1. Scenic Cruising:

One of the highlights of an Alaska cruise is the opportunity to experience breathtaking scenic cruising along the Inside Passage, Glacier Bay, Hubbard Glacier, and other iconic routes. Passengers can witness stunning landscapes, towering fjords, and calving glaciers from the comfort of the ship's decks or observation lounges.

2. Wildlife Viewing:

Alaska's abundant wildlife offers fantastic opportunities for passengers to spot marine mammals, such as whales, seals, and sea lions, as well as bald eagles, bears, and other indigenous species. Many cruise lines have naturalists or wildlife experts on board to provide insights and help passengers identify wildlife during their journey.

3. Educational Programs:

To enhance the cruise experience, many ships offer educational programs and enrichment activities related to Alaska's culture, history, and natural environment. This may include onboard lectures, workshops, and interactive presentations conducted by experts in fields such as marine biology, indigenous cultures, and geology.

4. Culinary Experiences:

Alaska cruises often feature regional cuisine and dining experiences that showcase local flavors and ingredients. Passengers can savor Alaskan seafood, such as wild salmon and king crab, as well as other specialties inspired by the region's culinary heritage.

5. Entertainment:

Cruise ships provide a range of entertainment options, including live music performances, theater shows, comedy acts, and themed events. Passengers can enjoy Broadway-style productions, guest performers, and engaging entertainment tailored to the Alaska cruise experience.

6. Onboard Activities:

From fitness classes and sports facilities to art auctions and craft workshops, cruise ships offer a diverse array of onboard activities to suit different interests. Passengers can participate in activities such as yoga classes, wine tastings, trivia contests, and dance lessons while at sea.

7. Spa and Wellness:

For relaxation and rejuvenation, cruise ships feature spa facilities offering a range of treatments, massages, and wellness services. Passengers can unwind in saunas, steam rooms, or hot tubs while taking in scenic views of the Alaskan coastline.

8. Shopping:

Onboard boutiques and duty-free shops provide opportunities for passengers to indulge in retail therapy and purchase souvenirs, jewelry, clothing, and Alaskan-themed gifts. Guests can browse for unique items and mementos to commemorate their cruise experience.

9. Family-Friendly Activities:

Alaska cruises cater to families with children by offering dedicated kids' clubs, youth programs, and family-friendly activities. These may include supervised play areas, interactive games, movie nights, and special events designed for younger passengers.

10. Social Spaces:

Cruise ships feature various social spaces where passengers can relax and socialize with fellow travelers. This includes lounges, bars, coffee shops, and outdoor deck areas that provide opportunities for mingling and enjoying the company of other guests.

11. Enrichment Programs:

Some cruise lines offer enrichment programs focused on Alaska's culture and heritage. This may involve onboard demonstrations of traditional crafts, storytelling sessions by local experts, or hands-on experiences that provide insights into the region's traditions.

12. Outdoor Recreation:

Outdoor enthusiasts can take advantage of the ship's amenities for outdoor recreation, such as jogging tracks, sports courts, or even rock climbing walls. Additionally, some ships offer guided nature walks or outdoor adventure excursions when docked at ports of call.

Chapter 6: How to Get Around Alaska

It takes careful planning and consideration of your transportation options to set off on an adventure through Alaska's breathtaking scenery. With its enormous peaks and breathtaking glaciers, the Last Frontier is a place of wonders.

As you set out on your Alaskan adventure, the journey begins with thoughtful planning, encompassing the selection of suitable lodging and an assessment of transportation modes that promise to reveal the natural beauty of the state. Transportation in Alaska is not merely a means to an end; it becomes an integral part of the experience, effortlessly connecting you with awe-inspiring scenery, diverse cultures, and countless experiences waiting to be uncovered in this pristine wilderness.

Cruise Ships

Cruise ships stand as the principal and arguably most alluring means of transportation for those yearning to explore Alaska's stunning scenery up close. Renowned cruise lines craft meticulously designed itineraries that unfold like a tapestry, with calls at several ports in Alaska, including the breathtaking Denali, Glacier Bay, and Skagway. Beyond mere convenience, cruises offer a captivating show, treating passengers to sweeping vistas of glaciers, pristine fjords, and the rugged landscapes that define this untamed wilderness.

Rail Travel

Rail travel in Alaska presents a scenic and comfortable alternative, allowing you to explore the heart of the state. The iconic Alaska Railroad offers panoramic views of mountains, forests, and wildlife. Whether you're heading to Denali National Park to witness the towering peak of North America's highest mountain or exploring the charming town of Talkeetna, the railway provides a unique perspective on Alaska's vast and diverse interior.

Small Aircraft and Bush Planes

For those seeking to reach remote areas with limited road access, small aircraft and bush planes become essential companions. Soaring above Alaska's expansive landscapes, these flights offer breathtaking views of glaciers, mountains, and untouched wilderness. Beyond being a mode of transportation, these aerial experiences provide an unparalleled opportunity to witness the grandeur of Alaska from the skies.

Car Rentals

Renting a car in Alaska opens the door to unparalleled freedom, allowing you to explore the state's vast highways, scenic byways, and national parks at your own pace. Take a road trip along the Alaska Highway, Dalton Highway, or Seward Highway for a firsthand encounter with the state's diverse geography, abundant wildlife, and charming small towns.

Ferries

The Alaska Marine Highway System connects coastal communities and islands, providing a unique way to explore the state by sea. Ferries offer a relaxed and scenic journey, allowing you to discover the coastal charm of Alaskan communities and islands. Island hopping becomes a delightful part of the adventure, with each ferry ride unveiling new coastal treasures.

Bush Travel and Dog Sledding

In remote regions, bush travel and dog sledding offer exciting and authentic ways to experience traditional Alaskan transportation. Whether you're mushing through the snow or flying in a bush plane, these experiences immerse you in Alaska's rich history and adventurous spirit, providing a deep connection with the state's cultural roots.

Chapter 7: Accommodation Options Around Alaska

When visiting the Last Frontier, visitors find a wide variety of accommodation choices that mirror the diversity of Alaska's terrain. Cozy cottages and isolated wilderness lodges beckon, each offering a unique window into the state's raw charm. These lodgings offer a wide variety of experiences that let travelers fully appreciate Alaska's wild splendor. For anyone looking to experience the genuine spirit of Alaska's appeal, these accommodations, whether tucked away in picturesque nooks or tucked deep into the wilderness, promise an amazing voyage. Discover the state's hospitality against the majestic backdrop of nature, guaranteeing an unforgettable experience each and every time you visit.

1. Wilderness Lodges:

In the midst of unexplored regions, Alaska's wilderness lodges serve as landmarks. These lodges, which are located in remote areas, provide an immersive natural experience that lets visitors escape the outside world. Beautiful views of glaciers, mountains, and wildlife are frequently available from the cozy yet rustic cabins. Surrounded by the breathtaking splendor of Alaska's wild wilderness, guests can enjoy the peace and quiet of their surroundings.

2. Hotels and Resorts:

Anchorage, Fairbanks, and Juneau are among the cities where travelers can find a range of hotels and resorts. Whether seeking the convenience of urban amenities or a touch of luxury after a day of exploration, these accommodations cater to diverse preferences. Visitors can choose from upscale hotels with modern conveniences or opt for more intimate lodgings that reflect the local character and hospitality of Alaska.

3. Vacation Rentals:

Vacation rentals, including cabins, cottages, and remote lodges, offer a more private and personalized stay. This option allows travelers to tailor their Alaskan experience, with properties scattered throughout the state. From coastal cabins with panoramic views to secluded cottages nestled in the wilderness, these rentals provide a home away from home amid Alaska's stunning scenery.

4. Bed & Breakfasts:

Numerous bed & breakfasts operated by hospitable residents can be found throughout Alaska's small towns and villages. These accommodations provide a cozy, one-on-one experience, with hosts offering insights into the local way of life and suggesting must-see hidden attractions. A substantial breakfast is provided to guests before they set off on their Alaskan excursions, fostering a sense of camaraderie and connection.

5. Campgrounds and RV Parks:

For the adventurous souls seeking an authentic outdoor experience, Alaska's extensive network of campgrounds and RV parks beckons. Whether pitching a tent in Denali National Park or parking an RV along the scenic coastline, camping provides an opportunity to immerse oneself in the natural beauty of Alaska, with starlit nights and the sounds of nature as companions.

6. Fishing Lodges:

Alaska's reputation as a premier fishing destination is reflected in its fishing lodges strategically located near prime fishing spots. These lodges not only offer comfortable accommodations but also provide guided fishing expeditions, creating an ideal setting for anglers seeking both adventure and relaxation. Guests can enjoy the thrill of reeling in salmon or halibut, surrounded by the breathtaking Alaskan wilderness.

7. Cabins and Cottages:

Throughout Alaska, especially in more remote areas, travelers can find an abundance of cabins and cottages available for rent. From simple and secluded cabins in the woods to waterfront cottages offering panoramic views, these accommodations provide a cozy and intimate setting for a memorable Alaskan getaway. Guests can unwind by the fireplace or stargaze from the porch, surrounded by the tranquility of nature.

8. Glacier-View Lodging:

In regions like Kenai Fjords National Park and Glacier Bay, accommodations with glacier views are in high demand. Lodges and cabins strategically positioned to showcase the breathtaking beauty of glaciers offer a unique and awe-inspiring experience. Guests can wake up to the sight of towering ice formations, creating memories that will last a lifetime.

9. Unique Wilderness Experiences:

For those seeking a touch of novelty, Alaska offers unique wilderness experiences such as treehouse stays, yurts, or floating cabins. These unconventional accommodations provide an extraordinary way to connect with Alaska's untamed nature while still enjoying a comfortable stay. Guests can sleep amidst the treetops or on the gentle waves, adding an element of adventure to their Alaskan sojourn.

10. Remote Huts and Cabins:

In Alaska's vast backcountry, remote huts and cabins are scattered, offering a more rugged and secluded experience. Accessible by hiking, skiing, or small aircraft, these off-the-grid accommodations provide an opportunity for solitude and immersion in the wilderness. Guests can forge their own path, surrounded by the pristine beauty of Alaska's untouched landscapes.

Chapter 8: Outdoor Activities To Experience On Land

For those who enjoy the great outdoors, the Alaska Range's towering peaks and the Inside Passage's frozen fjords provide a striking background. Traveling across Alaska's wild areas reveals a wide range of outdoor pursuits on land. Encounters with the majesty of nature can be had via hiking across wide, unspoiled areas, kayaking among glaciers, or wildlife viewing in Denali National Park. A celestial show is added to the already stunning scenery as the Northern Lights dance across the Arctic sky. Alaska's wild charm draws people looking for unmatched experiences in a place where nature rules supreme, whether that adventure be dog sledding through snowy slopes or fishing in isolated rivers. A voyage of exploration and a meeting with the unadulterated, raw spirit of the Last Frontier are promised by this enormous and varied terrain.

1. Glacier Exploration:

Alaska is synonymous with glaciers, and exploring these massive ice formations is an unforgettable experience. The Mendenhall Glacier in Juneau and the Hubbard Glacier in Yakutat Bay are just a glimpse into the state's glacial wonders. Travelers can partake in guided glacier hikes, ice climbing adventures, or even take a helicopter ride for a breathtaking aerial view of these icy giants.

2. Hiking and Backpacking:

Alaska's vast wilderness is crisscrossed with an extensive network of trails catering to all levels of hikers. Denali National Park offers a range of hiking options, from short walks to challenging backcountry routes with stunning views of North America's tallest peak. The historic Chilkoot Trail, following the Klondike Gold Rush route, offers a unique blend of history and wilderness exploration.

3. Fishing:

For anglers, Alaska is a paradise with its pristine rivers and abundant marine life. The Kenai River is famous for salmon fishing, Cook Inlet offers thrilling halibut fishing, and Bristol Bay is a haven for fly fishing enthusiasts. Whether casting a line from the shoreline or chartering a boat for a deep-sea excursion, the opportunities for a rewarding catch are abundant.

4. Northern Lights Viewing:

Alaska's high latitudes make it one of the best places on Earth to witness the Northern Lights. During the winter months, particularly in places like Fairbanks, the sky comes alive with vibrant hues of green and pink. Guided tours or venturing out on your own to remote locations provide optimal viewing conditions for this celestial phenomenon.

5. Kayaking and Rafting:

The state's numerous rivers and coastal waters offer ideal conditions for kayaking and rafting adventures. Paddle through serene fjords, navigate glacial lakes, or brave the exhilarating rapids of rivers like the Nenana. Kayaking allows for an up-close exploration of Alaska's waterways, providing unique perspectives on its stunning landscapes.

6. Flightseeing Tours:

Embark on a thrilling flightseeing tour to witness Alaska's vastness from the air. Small aircraft or helicopters offer breathtaking views of glaciers, mountains, and remote wilderness areas inaccessible by road. Soar over the Misty Fjords National Monument or gaze upon the expansive beauty of Denali, experiencing the state's grandeur in a way that few get to.

7. Dog Sledding:

Experience the timeless tradition of dog sledding against the backdrop of Alaska's winter wonderland. Whether on a glacier or through snow-covered forests, dog sledding tours provide a unique and exhilarating way to explore the state's snowy landscapes. Meet teams of enthusiastic sled dogs and skilled mushers who bring this iconic Alaskan activity to life.

8. Camping and RVing:

For those seeking an authentic Alaskan adventure, camping and RVing offer a way to immerse oneself in the wilderness. Set up camp amidst towering mountains and pristine lakes, with many state and national parks providing camping facilities. This allows visitors to forge a deeper connection with nature in a more intimate setting.

9. Cultural Immersion:

Delve into Alaska's rich cultural tapestry by visiting museums, attending cultural events, and exploring traditional villages. Learn about the traditions of the Inupiat, Yupik, Athabascan, and other indigenous peoples, gaining insights into their history, art, and customs. Engage with local communities to understand the ongoing connection between Alaska's residents and their environment.

Chapter 9: Sightseeing

Historic Sites and Museums

Setting out on an Alaska cruise unveils a unique opportunity to delve into the rich historical legacy of the Last Frontier. From Juneau to Skagway, each port of call offers an array of historic sites and museums that not only chronicle the state's vibrant past but also seamlessly integrate with the breathtaking natural landscapes. Exploring these selected historic sites during your Alaska cruise promises a captivating blend of natural wonders and cultural heritage. It offers a well-rounded and immersive experience, allowing travelers to not only witness the stunning landscapes but also connect with the intricate stories that have shaped this awe-inspiring region over the centuries. Let's take an extended journey through these meticulously chosen locales.

In Juneau

1. Alaska State Museum:

Nestled in Juneau, the Alaska State Museum is a veritable treasure trove of Alaskan history and culture. Beyond the mere display of artifacts, historical photographs, and interactive exhibits, this museum offers visitors a profound glimpse into the diverse heritage that defines the state. From Native Alaskan traditions to the nuances of the gold rush era, the Alaska State Museum is a comprehensive exploration of Alaska's multifaceted past.

2. Mendenhall Glacier Visitor Center:

While not a conventional museum, the Mendenhall Glacier Visitor Center in Juneau seamlessly weaves geological knowledge with historical perspectives. Enabling visitors to witness the majestic Mendenhall Glacier, the center imparts insights into the impact of glaciers on the region. It's a holistic educational experience that combines the awe-inspiring beauty of nature with the scientific understanding of its historical context.

3. Last Chance Mining Museum:

Housed in Juneau's historic compressor building, the Last Chance Mining Museum is a captivating journey into the gold mining history of the region. The artifacts and exhibits vividly portray the challenges faced by miners during the gold rush era, making it a living testament to Juneau's golden legacy.

In Ketchikan

1. Totem Bight State Historical Park:

Ketchikan's Totem Bight State Historical Park immerses visitors in the intricate artistry and symbolism of Native Alaskan tribes. Beyond the awe-inspiring collection of totem poles, guided tours provide a deep historical context, connecting the dots between the carvings and the vibrant traditions of the indigenous people.

2. Dolly's House Museum:

Offering a fascinating insight into the history of Creek Street, Ketchikan's former red-light district, Dolly's House Museum stands as a preserved historic site. It not only showcases the colorful past of this waterfront area but also encapsulates the social and economic dynamics of Ketchikan during a pivotal period.

3. Southeast Alaska Discovery Center:

Serving as a comprehensive hub for understanding the ecology and cultural history of the region, the Southeast Alaska Discovery Center in Ketchikan is a beacon of knowledge. From the vast Tongass National Forest to the intricate traditions of Native Alaskans, the exhibits provide a nuanced perspective on the diverse ecosystems that define Southeast Alaska.

In Sitka

1. Sitka National Historical Park:

Preserving the battleground of a critical 1804 clash between Russian settlers and the Tlingit people, Sitka National Historical Park is a testament to Alaska's complex history. The Totem Trail and the Russian Bishop's House offer a multifaceted exploration, blending Native Alaskan heritage with the remnants of Alaska's Russian colonial past.

2. Russian-American Building #29:

Also known as the Baranov Museum, this historic building in Sitka was once a residence for Russian-American Company officials. Now, it serves as a captivating repository of exhibits detailing Sitka's Russian colonial period, providing a window into the region's fur trade and cultural evolution.

3. Sheet'ká Kwáan Naa Kahídi Community House:

Functioning as a cultural center and museum, the Sheet'ká Kwáan Naa Kahídi Community House in Sitka delves into the traditions and art of the indigenous Tlingit people. The exhibits, featuring ceremonial regalia and traditional art, offer a profound understanding of the rich cultural heritage of the Tlingit.

In Skagway

1. Klondike Gold Rush National Historical Park:

Skagway's pivotal role in the Klondike Gold Rush is immortalized in the Klondike Gold Rush National Historical Park. With meticulously restored buildings, engaging exhibits, and insightful walking tours, this park provides a tangible link to the challenges faced by gold rush prospectors, encapsulating a crucial chapter in Alaska's history.

2. Skagway Museum and Archives:

The Skagway Museum and Archives unravel the town's gold rush history, placing it within the broader context of Alaska's development. Through a curated collection of artifacts, photographs, and personal stories, the museum provides an intimate look into the lives of those who shaped Skagway during this transformative era.

Monuments and Memorials

An Alaska cruise is a voyage through breathtaking landscapes, but it also offers the chance to encounter monuments and memorials that reflect the region's history, culture, and natural wonders. While Alaska may not be known for traditional monuments in the way that some destinations are, there are significant sites that commemorate its rich heritage and pay homage to its unique identity. From war memorials to totem poles, each site contributes to the narrative of Alaska's past and present, offering cruise passengers a deeper understanding of the unique heritage that defines this remarkable destination.

1. Alaska Veterans Memorial:

Located in Juneau, the Alaska Veterans Memorial honors the state's military members who have served in various conflicts. The monument includes statues representing each branch of the military, offering a solemn tribute to the sacrifices made by Alaskan servicemen and women.

2. Captain Cook Monument:

In Resurrection Bay near Seward, the Captain Cook
Monument commemorates the famous explorer's
visits to the region in the 18th century. The
monument is a tribute to the early European
explorers who mapped and documented Alaska's
coast.

3. Nome's Gold Rush Cemetery:

While Nome is renowned for its Gold Rush history, the Gold Rush Cemetery stands as a somber reminder of the challenges faced by those seeking fortune. Visitors can explore grave markers dating back to the late 19th century, capturing the essence of this historic era.

4. Alaska Native Heritage Center:

Located in Anchorage, the Alaska Native Heritage Center isn't just a monument but a living cultural institution. It offers immersive experiences, showcasing the diverse traditions, languages, and lifestyles of Alaska Native people, providing a deep understanding of their enduring legacy.

5. Fort Abercrombie State Historical Park:

On Kodiak Island, Fort Abercrombie State Historical Park includes remnants of World War II coastal defense installations. This park serves as a monument to the wartime history of Alaska and provides stunning views of the surrounding landscapes.

Recommended itinerary for first-timers

The first time you go on an Alaskan cruise, you'll have an amazing time with lots of different sights and breathtaking scenery. The area offers a number of suggested itineraries that combine breathtaking cruises, close encounters with wildlife, cultural immersions, and exhilarating outdoor experiences to suit the diverse interests of tourists. Here is a thorough suggested itinerary that highlights the best that the Alaskan wilderness has to offer for individuals making their first trip there:

Day 1: Departure from Seattle or Vancouver

Commence your Alaskan journey by boarding your cruise ship in either Seattle, Washington, or Vancouver, British Columbia. As you set sail, soak in the breathtaking views of the Pacific Northwest, anticipating the rugged coastline and untamed beauty of Alaska that lies ahead.

Day 2: Inside Passage

Embark on a full day of scenic cruising through the renowned Inside Passage, a mesmerizing network of fjords, channels, and islands celebrated for its lush rainforests, majestic mountains, and prolific wildlife. Keep your eyes peeled for whales, eagles, and other marine wonders in this pristine wilderness.

Day 3: Juneau

Arrive in Alaska's capital city, Juneau, where a myriad of experiences awaits. Explore the spectacular Mendenhall Glacier, ascend Mount Roberts via tram for panoramic vistas, or partake in a whale-watching excursion to witness humpback whales in their natural habitat.

Day 4: Skagway

Transport yourself back to the Klondike Gold Rush era in the historic town of Skagway. Ride the White Pass & Yukon Route Railroad, visit the Klondike Gold Rush National Historical Park, or embark on a hike along the Chilkoot Trail, immersing yourself in frontier history and breathtaking scenery.

Day 5: Glacier Bay National Park

Marvel at the awe-inspiring beauty of Glacier Bay National Park, a UNESCO World Heritage site renowned for its towering glaciers, calving icebergs, and untouched wilderness. Listen to the thunderous crack of ice as your ship navigates through this dramatic and pristine landscape.

Day 6: Ketchikan

Immerse yourself in Native American culture and discover the "Salmon Capital of the World" in

Ketchikan. Visit Totem Bight State Historical Park, witness a traditional Tlingit dance performance, or embark on a floatplane excursion to the Misty Fjords National Monument.

Day 7: Victoria, British Columbia

Conclude your Alaskan adventure with a stop in Victoria, British Columbia. Explore the charming city's historic architecture, lush gardens, and vibrant waterfront. Don't miss the iconic Butchart Gardens or a visit to the majestic Fairmont Empress Hotel.

Day 8: Return to Seattle or Vancouver

As your cruise draws to a close, disembark in Seattle or Vancouver, carrying with you indelible memories of an unforgettable Alaskan adventure.

This painstakingly designed itinerary guarantees a harmonious fusion of natural wonders, cultural richness, and plenty of outdoor exploration options, offering a thorough introduction to the pleasures of an Alaskan cruise. An Alaskan cruise ensures first-time visitors to this amazing region a wealth of unique experiences, regardless of their interests in glaciers, wildlife, history, or indigenous traditions.

Making the Most of Your Cruise

Insider Tips for Alaska Cruisers

Setting out on an Alaskan cruise is an incredible journey, and astute insider advice can greatly enhance your total enjoyment. It's critical to comprehend the peculiar weather dynamics. Layered gear, such as thermal layers, waterproof outerwear, and sturdy footwear, are necessary for comfort in Alaska's erratic climate, where sunshine and rain can change rapidly.

Make sure you have a good camera and binoculars so you can fully enjoy the breathtaking scenery and plethora of species. These are quite helpful for taking pictures of the glaciers and various species, such as bears, eagles, and whales, during scenic sailing and beach excursions.

Thorough preparation is essential; look into and reserve shore excursions ahead of time to get coveted spaces on popular tours and ensure you have the chance to participate in activities that interest you. The balcony suites offer wildlife aficionados a private view of Alaska's breathtaking environment without having to deal with crowded decks, which will appeal to them.

Formal nights offer an opportunity to dress up for special dinners and gatherings and are a regular feature on Alaskan cruises. If you plan on attending these sophisticated events, make sure to pack appropriately with cocktail dresses, suits, or formal attire.

Beyond clothing, savor regional food while on board, investigate cultural enrichment through historians, naturalists, and cultural specialists giving onboard lectures, and converse with the ship's naturalists to get knowledge of Alaska's fauna, flora, and geological aspects. Remain adaptable when creating your itinerary, keeping in mind that the weather sometimes calls for changes. Take motion sickness precautions into consideration, especially in choppy waters close to glaciers.

Photography Tips for Capturing Alaska's Beauty

Exploring the diverse and awe-inspiring landscapes of Alaska through photography requires a thoughtful approach. Thorough research of specific locations, including scenic spots, wildlife habitats, and cultural landmarks, is essential for planning successful photography outings. When packing for the journey, prioritize versatile gear, such as a camera with interchangeable lenses wide-angle for expansive landscapes and telephoto for wildlife. A sturdy tripod ensures stability in various conditions, while protective gear is crucial for Alaska's rapidly changing weather.

Given Alaska's northern latitude, the sunlight creates unique conditions, especially during the extended daylight hours of summer. Strategic timing during the golden hours of sunrise and sunset enhances the natural beauty of the landscape with warm, soft light. Photographing wildlife demands respect for their safety; maintaining a distance and using telephoto lenses is essential. Patience is key during wildlife encounters, requiring time for observation and capturing the perfect shot.

The reflective surfaces of Alaska's lakes and fjords offer opportunities for capturing mirror-like reflections, adding depth to images. Embracing the weather variability, from clear skies to fog or rain, adds drama and atmosphere to photographs. Including elements like people or structures in compositions provides scale and context, emphasizing the vastness of Alaska's grand landscapes. Post-processing techniques, including adjusting exposure and color balance, enhance the full potential of images.

Souvenirs for Cruisers

Stopping at a variety of shops is a worthwhile task in order to pick up sentimental souvenirs when taking a cruise across Alaska's scenery. Whether these shops are tucked away from well-known cruise lines, neighborhood shops, or art galleries, Alaska provides a diverse selection of souvenirs that encapsulate the state's amazing natural beauty and native cultures. These souvenirs appeal to a diverse spectrum of tastes, from those who enjoy the outdoors and wildlife to those who want physical remembrances of their amazing cruise experience.

Discover some well-known souvenirs in Alaska:

- Native Art: Totems, masks, and jewelry — Alaska's soul in handcrafted heritage.
- Wildlife Treasures: Bears, eagles, and whales on vivid souvenirs, nature's keepsakes.
- Alaskan Bling: Jade, gold, and native designs wear the spirit of the North.
- Ulu Blades: Traditional knives, symbolic and functional echoes of Alaska's past.
- Wild Wearables: T-shirts, hats, scarves, Alaska's icons on you.
- Frozen Moments: Photography prints, Alaska's grandeur in snapshots.
- Tasty Memories: Smoked salmon, jams, and birch syrup, flavors of the Last Frontier.

- Artistic Pottery: Ceramics adorned with wildlife, Alaska's beauty in every piece.

By exploring these souvenir options, cruisers can find treasures that resonate with the unique character of Alaska's landscapes, wildlife, and indigenous cultures. Each item serves as a tangible memory, encapsulating the spirit of their remarkable cruise journey through Alaska's awe-inspiring wonders.

Chapter 10: Sailing Around Some Other Ports In and Out of Alaska with Maps

Overview of Seattle

Known as the "Emerald City," Seattle is a bustling city in the stunning Pacific Northwest region of the United States. Specifically, it is in the state of Washington, on the western coast of the country.

Seattle, which is well-known for its distinct fusion of technological innovation, urban sophistication, and breathtaking natural scenery, is a prime example of how history and modernity can coexist together.

The story of this city began to change in the middle of the 19th century when European settlers arrived, bringing with them roots well ingrained in the customs of the Coast Salish peoples. Today, Seattle is known for its unapologetic acceptance of ethnic diversity and inventiveness. The city's dynamic personality is shaped in part by its strong innovation tradition, maritime background, and active arts scene.

Puget Sound provides a tranquil backdrop, and Seattle is surrounded by the magnificent Olympic and Cascade mountain ranges, making its natural environment nothing short of magnificent. Parks, lush vegetation, and iconic sites like Discovery Park encourage locals and tourists to get outdoors.

The city's thriving technology industry, which is home to multinational behemoths like Microsoft, Amazon, and Boeing, is the engine of its economy. Seattle's dedication to environmental sustainability, which places a strong emphasis on public transit, renewable energy, and eco-friendly urban development, has also won it praise.

Seattle is a well-liked place to start Alaskan cruises, and it provides a taste of a variety of adventures. Every neighborhood, from the diverse Capitol Hill to the historic Pioneer Square, contributes a different character to the city. Seattle's reputation as the best place to begin an Alaskan cruise is further cemented by its vibrant food scene, which offers a variety of international cuisines and cutting-edge eating options. Essentially, Seattle's diverse appeal entices discovery, striking a balance between history and contemporary appeal in an enthralling cityscape.

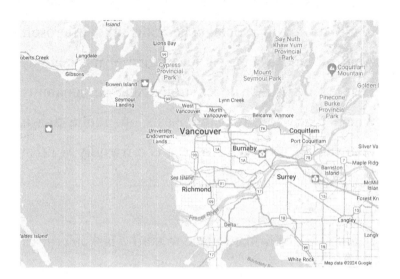

Overview of Vancouver

Vancouver, located in the picturesque province of British Columbia, is not only a major global center renowned for its natural beauty, cultural diversity, and high standard of living, but it also acts as a crucial starting point for travelers who want to experience the exciting adventure of an Alaskan cruise. The city's rich history is enriched with a rich cultural backdrop that is unique to the area and adds to the entire experience of tourists. These peoples include the Musqueam, Squamish, and Tsleil-Waututh Nations.

Established in 1886, Vancouver has grown into an internationally recognized center, a vibrant metropolis seamlessly blending history and modernity. Its multicultural tapestry is on vivid display in neighborhoods like Chinatown, Little India, and Punjabi Market, reflecting a harmonious fusion of traditions from around the globe. Vancouver's commitment to green spaces is exemplified by the iconic Stanley Park, a verdant oasis featuring lush forests, scenic seawalls, and emblematic totem poles, creating an ideal prelude to the awe-inspiring landscapes awaiting Alaska-bound travelers.

Its prime location, providing quick access to the Pacific Ocean and the unspoiled nature of the northern border, highlights Vancouver's importance as a starting point for Alaska cruises. The North Shore mountains are close by, giving cruise passengers an idea of the grand view they might expect. Outdoor enthusiasts will enjoy the abundance of activities available against the stunning backdrop of the city.

In addition to being a major economic force, Vancouver's thriving economy is also a vibrant center that fosters an adventurous spirit. It is fueled by sectors including biotechnology, technology, filmmaking, and green innovation. Alaska cruise fans frequently embrace an ecologically sensitive mindset, and the city's commitment to sustainability is shown in its aggressive aims for lowering carbon emissions and supporting eco-friendly practices.

A vibrant atmosphere is created by culturally rich events like the Vancouver International Film Festival and the Celebration of Light fireworks competition, which offer an extra layer of intrigue and capture guests before they go for their Alaskan adventure. Travelers heading out on their journey will find Vancouver to be an invaluable starting point due to its seamless fusion of natural grandeur, vibrant culture, and urban sophistication. This will make the trip to Alaska's pristine landscapes an unforgettable prelude, beginning here on the West Coast.

Overview of Anchorage

Anchorage is the largest city in Alaska, emerging as a vibrant urban center with roots extending back thousands of years, enriched by a diverse tapestry of cultures and traditions within its population of over 290,000. Nestled between the Chugach Mountains and the ocean, Anchorage's strategic location not only offers breathtaking vistas but also serves as a gateway to a plethora of outdoor adventures. The city's economic vitality is fueled by diverse industries, including oil, transportation, tourism, healthcare, and government services, underscoring its significance in the Alaskan landscape.

Culturally, Anchorage comes alive with events and festivals that pay homage to the rugged Alaskan wilderness. From the exhilarating Fur Rendezvous winter festival to the iconic Iditarod Trail Sled Dog Race, the city vibrates with the spirit of its surroundings. Anchorage's downtown area, a bustling hub of activity, invites exploration with its array of shops, restaurants, and cultural attractions. The Anchorage Museum stands as a testament to the city's commitment to preserving and showcasing Alaskan art, history, and culture through its extensive collections and engaging exhibits.

For a deeper immersion into Alaska's rich heritage, the Alaska Native Heritage Center provides an interactive experience that highlights the traditions and customs of Alaska Native peoples. Outdoor enthusiasts are spoiled for choice, with opportunities for hiking, wildlife viewing, camping, and heli-skiing in the winter. The Alyeska Resort in Girdwood offers world-class skiing and snowboarding experiences against a backdrop of stunning landscapes.

The variety of its cultural influences and availability of locally grown food are reflected in Anchorage's culinary scene. In celebration of Alaskan customs and the outdoor lifestyle of the area, the city organizes yearly festivals and events such the Fur Rendezvous Festival, Summer Solstice Festival, and Anchorage International Film Festival. Travelers are drawn to Anchorage by its appealing combination of metropolitan conveniences and close proximity to unspoiled wilderness, which offers them the chance to experience adventure, cultural discovery, and a deep connection to the wild grandeur of the natural world.

Chapter 11: Health and Safety Precautions

Safety Precautions

Taking the time to familiarize oneself with the ship's layout upon boarding is crucial, including locating emergency exits, lifeboats, and life jackets. Attending safety briefings and adhering to instructions from the ship's crew, such as participating in mandatory safety drills and heeding safety-related announcements, is imperative. Alaska's unpredictable weather necessitates packing appropriately, with consideration for rain gear, warm layers, and sturdy footwear for shore excursions.

Respecting the natural environment and adhering to guidelines provided by tour operators during wildlife viewing activities is essential, maintaining a safe distance and refraining from approaching or feeding wild animals. Given Alaska's deceptively sunny climate, staying hydrated and applying sunscreen regularly, particularly during outdoor activities, is vital. Monitoring weather forecasts and staying flexible to adapt to rapid weather changes in certain areas of Alaska is equally important.

When exploring ports of call, practicing safe behavior, staying with your group, and being aware of your surroundings are crucial on shore excursions. Exercise caution in glacier areas, following the guidance of experienced guides due to the unpredictability of these natural wonders. Should any health concerns or injuries arise during the cruise, seeking medical assistance from the ship's medical staff or local facilities at ports of call is advised.

Security On Excursion

Another thing travelers can enjoy on this Alaskan cruise is a wide range of fascinating shore excursions, from wildlife watching to glacier trekking and immersive cultural experiences, when they set sail on an Alaskan cruise. These excursions provide travelers with an opportunity to fully immerse themselves in Alaska's unique culture and breathtaking scenery. But even with the allure of these experiences, security and safety must come first. Following specific instructions is essential for a safe and satisfying experience.

First and foremost, before making any reservations for shore excursions, would-be explorers should thoroughly investigate reliable tour companies. It is crucial to choose businesses that are insured, licensed, and have knowledgeable guides committed to the safety of their passengers. In order to add even more protection and comfort, cruise lines frequently provide a choice of approved shore excursions via reliable partners.

It is essential that you pay close attention to any safety instructions given by tour guides or ship officials before embarking on any trip. Important details regarding emergency methods, safety precautions, and expectations for the excursion are covered in these briefings. To reduce the chance of getting lost or running into danger, it is crucial to stay with the group and follow the tour guide's directions while on the excursion.

It is also important to keep a safe distance when going on wildlife viewing excursions because Alaska is home to a broad range of animals, such as bears, moose, and marine mammals. Basic safety measures include dressing appropriately for the weather and terrain, packing necessities like water, snacks, sunscreen, insect repellent, and prescription drugs, and using caution when near glaciers by adhering to the guide's directions.

When going on excursions, it's also a good idea to keep a watchful eye on personal possessions and avoid bringing valuables or big sums of cash. It is possible to reduce the chance of theft by using a secure bag or backpack. It is advisable to raise any queries you may have regarding the security of an expedition, as tour guides are there to guarantee safety and provide information. The final step in creating a safe and unforgettable Alaskan cruise experience is to have emergency contact information for the cruise ship or local authorities in case of unanticipated circumstances.

Emergency services

In order to guarantee the safety of guests and crew in the event of medical emergencies, natural disasters, or unanticipated incidents, emergency services are an essential part of an Alaskan cruise. Cruise lines in Alaska that operate under strict rules create elaborate emergency response plans that can handle a range of situations. A variety of medical services, from basic first aid to specialized care, are provided by medical facilities on board cruise ships operating in Alaskan seas. These facilities are manned by licensed physicians and nurses. Provisions for emergency medical evacuations are in place in the event of serious medical situations that exceed on-board capabilities. This guarantees that patients are flown or transferred by sea to the closest appropriate medical facility.

Competent crew members who make up trained emergency response teams aboard cruise ships go through frequent training and drills to prepare them to manage a variety of events, including medical emergencies, fires, and evacuations. On-board communication systems help with coordination and contact with onshore authorities, such as the U.S. Coast Guard and local emergency services. To familiarize passengers with safety procedures, passenger safety drills that cover emergency evacuation methods and correct usage of life jackets are required.

Thorough emergency response plans prioritize everyone's safety by including protocols for medical emergencies, fires, extreme weather, and aboard events. Shore excursions follow safety guidelines, and cruise lines work with reliable tour operators to reduce hazards. Public address systems and security measures are features of cruise ships that facilitate clear communication in case of emergency and potential threats. Cruise lines work closely with local authorities to provide a strong framework for everyone's safety and security on board by giving passengers complete contact details for on-board medical facilities and emergency response teams.

Conclusion

As the final chapter of the "Alaska Cruise Travel Guide" unfolds, it leaves readers with more than tips and recommendations—it bequeaths them with a profound connection to Alaska's untamed beauty. This guide isn't just a manual; it's a passport to an extraordinary journey. Reflect on the wildlife encounters, cultural revelations, and breathtaking landscapes. Close the book, but let it be a stepping stone to new beginnings—an invitation to embrace the call of the Last Frontier once again. The voyage may end, but the story continues, etched in memories as enduring as the ancient glaciers themselves.